MILES BRADLEY
Emotional Dance Music

I0191222

BROKEN SLEEP BOOKS

Published 2020,
Broken Sleep Books:
Cornwall / Wales

brokensleepbooks.com

First Edition

Lay out your unrest.

Publisher/Editor: Aaron Kent
Editor: Charlie Baylis

Typeset in UK by Aaron Kent

Broken Sleep Books is committed to
a sustainable future for our planet,
and therefore uses print on
demand publication.

brokensleepbooks@gmail.com

ISBN: 978-1-913642-12-9

Contents

Good Morning, I Love You 7

The Definitive... (10) 8

The Definitive... (9) 9

Self Assessed Performance Review (You Could Keep

A Calendar) 10

The Definitive... (8) 11

The Definitive... (7) 12

End Credits for Absolutely Everything 13

The Definitive... (6) 14

The Definitive... (5) 15

Could Be Monsters 16

The Definitive... (4) 17

The Definitive... (3) 18

Every Gallery Ever 19

The Definitive... (2) 21

The Definitive... (1) 22

[excerpt from 'Falling Through Your Door Late

on the 24th/Listening to Audiobooks at Home

During Christmastime'] 23

Acknowledgements 25

For Hannah,
who understands.

Emotional Dance Music

Miles Bradley

Good Morning, I Love You

and you fall through space
and you fall through space
and you fall through space forever
until you stop somewhere to eat
and while your soup is cooling
you text me to say:
"I kind of, maybe,
am starting to sort of miss
waking up on a friend's floor
every once in a while.
I hope our thirties yield
a few more
dramatic discussions in bathtubs
at other people's parties.
I don't think that's so much to ask."
and you finish eating while watching the TV
which is showing a pretty good
silent, subtitled episode of King of the Hill
and you tidy up after yourself
and you open the door
and you are falling through space
and you are falling through space
and you are falling through space forever

The Definitive Publicly Voted Peer Reviewed Expert Assessed Ranking of Locations to Have Night Defining Year Wrecking Life Changing Conversations at House Parties

10.

A crowded kitchen at 11.30pm, all arms on the counter top, fourteen or more people finding their footing and the contact-happiness that comes with a firm hope that things will feel at least exactly this good until the sun rises and you go back to pretending there is anything more valuable than the time we spend with the people we choose to spend time with. But how the two of you communicate this is closer to - "I feel pretty good about this" "I do too" "I'm glad you're here" "I'm glad we're here"

The Definitive Publicly Voted Peer Reviewed Expert Assessed Ranking of Locations to Have Night Defining Year Wrecking Life Changing Conversations at House Parties

9.
The back garden, laying down in the grass at 6am, staring at the sky, side by side, unhurriedly letting go of a lot of things that one of you has wanted to hear and the other hasn't wanted to say.

Self Assessed Performance Review
(You Could Keep A Calendar)

you're really just a small bird
launching yourself into a wind tunnel
and hoping for the best.

you open your mouth
and let every piece of grit swirling around in there
pile on your tongue, and push it down
and keep it still.

you close your eyes and lock your wings
and let your body slam into ceiling and floor
and you remind yourself again and again

"well, there are worse things"

The Definitive Publicly Voted Peer Reviewed Expert Assessed Ranking of Locations to Have Night Defining Year Wrecking Life Changing Conversations at House Parties

8.

An attic bedroom, 10.45, both of you stood at the window, leaning out, watching through fading light as people that you love pair off and team up in the back garden and start to power up plans that have been in place for weeks and you talk about how much you both care about every single person you can see and when it started you weren't but by the time you decide to go downstairs you realise you're holding hands.

The Definitive Publicly Voted Peer Reviewed Expert Assessed Ranking of Locations to Have Night Defining Year Wrecking Life Changing Conversations at House Parties

7.
The walk there, 7-9pm, especially if it's through just the right part of the city / the suburbs / the town where you don't even need to think about it, you just know that every other group of people you pass is on their way to something they believe will be equally great, and you all emit a light and a heat and you all soak up the light and the heat and not even the one guy who says "let's just bail and go back to yours and watch funny videos" can sour your mood for even a second because you feel like everyone else in the postcode is saying: "ok. here we go."

End Credits for Absolutely Everything

I fake-casually, really-finally
approved of your groom and
you said: "One day
 we'll dance at your wedding too"

Years pass,
no one ever sees you,
and now I dream, a lot, actually,
about eating the last slice of coffee cake
from under the glass
in poorly lit bars
while all our friends sleep upstairs,
and I think I finally see the appeal
of so many dusky 50s ballads
and I make my peace

over and over.

A guy in a grey mask
at a book launch shoots me
in the shoulder
and as I black out he says:
"Sure, the solitary life
looks like it's working out
real well"

But I come to in the bathroom
with you cleaning up the wound
and telling me it'll be fine
glancing out the door to order a vodka soda
via a relay team of three to four friends
and in moments like this
I get more and more sure -

There will be no wedding,
but we will dance.

The Definitive Publicly Voted Peer Reviewed Expert Assessed Ranking of Locations to Have Night Defining Year Wrecking Life Changing Conversations at House Parties

6.

The neighbours back garden, laying down in the grass at 11pm, staring at the sky, side by side, ready to run if a light flicks on, almost hoping for the excuse to finally share a story with each other that's worth repeating to a third person.

The Definitive Publicly Voted Peer Reviewed Expert Assessed Ranking of Locations to Have Night Defining Year Wrecking Life Changing Conversations at House Parties

5.

A first floor bedroom, 1am, sat cross legged on a reasonably comfy bed, one of you assuring the other that there is still time for their night to turn around, and you really mean it and they really feel it and you bump cups, mugs, bottles, cans and you text the kid you think is in charge of the music right now and you tell them that it would be a really really good idea to hit your favourite person's favourite song sometime inside of the next fifteen and you tap send and look up and they are smiling and they say "can we hug first before we go back out?"

Could Be Monsters

He stops the car. He lowers the window. He smiles. She walks up to the car. She leans in the window. He asks if she is available right now. He asks if she wants to go somewhere else. She nods. He unlocks the door. She gets in the car.

He drives. She looks at the floor. He hands her an envelope. She opens it. She counts the money. She asks what he wants to do. He says the money is free. He says she doesn't have to do anything. He says he just wanted to do something nice, you know, for someone in need. He says at this time of year especially, you know, we need to look after each other. He says he has four frozen turkeys in the trunk. He says she can have one and he will drive her to wherever she lives and drop her off. He asks if it's enough money that she can stop working for the night. He asks if she wants a turkey. He says she doesn't have to do anything for the money or the food. He says she doesn't have to do anything at all.

She gives him an address. He drives. He says how he's not the richest guy in the world but he's doing ok right now. He says he can afford to do stuff like this to help people who need it. He says why not, right? He says if everyone who could afford to do this, did this then the world would just be a better place, you know? He waits at a red light. He looks at the sky. She looks at the floor.

He stops. He gets out of the car. He opens the trunk. He takes out a turkey. She gets out of the car. He gives the turkey to her. He hugs her. She flinches. She crumples. He gets back in the car. He watches her. She walks down the steps. She opens the door. She closes the door.
He adjusts the camera on his dashboard. He smiles straight into the camera on his dashboard. He turns off the camera on his dashboard.

The Definitive Publicly Voted Peer Reviewed Expert Assessed Ranking of Locations to Have Night Defining Year Wrecking Life Changing Conversations at House Parties

4.
Any corridor, landing, or other connecting space at 2am, the two of you taking a moment as a crowd (composed of: close old friends, recent additions, one girl's three really polite cousins who were in town for some family thing, your beloved arch-rival, adorable strangers) flows around and about, cuts from scene to scene and makes fifty movies that you two have just the tiniest role in and you lay out the script for that cameo and you shoot it and you both feel like you did some good, necessary work here before you split up and head out and promise to recombine later, knowing that there's a good chance you won't see them again for a very, very long time. You look up the spelling of 'coalesce' on your phone.

The Definitive Publicly Voted Peer Reviewed Expert Assessed Ranking of Locations to Have Night Defining Year Wrecking Life Changing Conversations at House Parties

3.
A large living room, 3am, arms around shoulders, mouths against ears, just after your mutually agreed on song of the summer finishes and the two of you fold into one while all around you the engine kicks in for the next thing and you like it but what you like more than that, more than anything except the feeling of giving your entire being over to the song that just ended - is this.

Every Gallery Ever

I no longer enjoy video art, because I always fear
it will suddenly erupt into graphic, distressing violence.

(It never does. Two European dancers whisper about air and
names as an amateur choir in the other room hits a high note
that reverberates right round the corner, the sound looking
for dark recesses to sink into but finding only bright white
walls. "So many monuments" they say, but I wouldn't mind
one more.)

On the other side of the city,
there is a miniature woodgrain staircase leading to nowhere
"I was hoping that was sculpture"
but all we get's inaccurate architecture
and forever still seismographs.
I am told that the "prominent dating undercuts the illusion
of representation"
making this a documentary film about a fallen kingdom that
a child imagined.

The internet will not tell me the name for a fear of paintings
but I have made myself sure that it is a phobia I had as a kid
– nothing should be so vast,
so vast that it won't fit into your field of vision.
It spreads everywhere and the colours aren't right because
real life is more monotone than anyone ever lets on.

With no natural light, I worry about power cuts.
What if the bleach bulbs fail and the CCTV cameras slip as
one into sleep
and it's just you and me and a canvas the size of my house
and a statue of a bull the size of a puppy?

I am lifted from the thought by:
"Does this resemble gravity?" the surtitles ask.

Choose your own adventure:

1. I'm not sure, sugar, but something's definitely bringing me down.

2. This three minute video loop will come back to me several hours later, as I step onto a train platform, and it will knock me down. I want so badly to go back and lay on the frozen floor, memorise the words then close my eyes and absorb the redirected sounds until I fix upon a meaning, until one of those moments of unintended synchronicity brings on a micro-epiphany. And I can leave the building with my head held high and the choir in the elevator will be all for me and I know I will have earned them.

3. It's not really ekphrasis, perhaps the best phrase is more like:
In every gallery ever,
there is a little bit of me
staring up at blank raised ceilings
whilst idle fingers underline pertinent portions
of Artist's Statements.

In every gallery ever
there is potential.
Take this space as your own
and use it for whatever you need.

I misquote, I paraphrase, the best bit was something like:

"If you were here
I would hold your breath for you"

The Definitive Publicly Voted Peer Reviewed Expert Assessed Ranking of Locations to Have Night Defining Year Wrecking Life Changing Conversations at House Parties

2.

A bathroom, door locked, at midnight, one of you sat on the toilet (seat down), one of you sat in the tub, both holding two drinks each, too locked in to the talk to really take in much of the noise of everyone else in the building rapidly nearing their peak, having the moment they will tell you about fifteen hours from now while you have this moment that you won't talk about for five years.

The Definitive Publicly Voted Peer Reviewed Expert Assessed Ranking of Locations to Have Night Defining Year Wrecking Life Changing Conversations at House Parties

1.
A cold, tiled kitchen floor at 5am. One of you sat with your back against the refrigerator door. One of you laying down. One of you speaking for a very long time, a lot more eloquent and even handed than you've ever been before, a lot more insightful and kind. The other nodding, smiling, very happy to stay here forever, or until everyone else goes home, which at times like this is basically the same thing.

[excerpt from 'Talling Through Your Door Late on the 24th/Listening to Audiobooks at Home During Christmastime']

despite the fact that you feel your heart sinking
steadily,
stopping at every floor
in the sixty-story building,

despite the fact that every time you breathe in
you take on a little of the anger
and the soot
and the overcrowding,

you still somehow radiate a tired,
gentle affection
for anyone
and anything that wants it.

you still somehow have a love that
interferes with phone signals
and throws off the GPS.

Acknowledgements

Thanks to Luke Kennard, whose tutelage, editing, sequencing suggestions and encouragement were vital to the creation of these poems. Thanks to Aaron Kent for his care and enthusiasm in making this a real physical object that exists in the world, and for everything he and Charlie Baylis do to run Britain's most emo press. Thanks to everyone who read and gave feedback on these poems in various forms 2009-2019: Rosie, Cait, Matt, Hannah C, Ashley, Kelly, Dan, Ed, Lin & Chelsey & Anaïs & Ian & Holly & everyone on Tumblr, Kate, Rachel, Anna, Jenna and Richard. Thanks to my parents for supporting my decision to not become a fighter pilot. Thanks to Jess, Jane, Alex, and Duncan for keeping my head above water. Thanks most of all to Hannah Tadd for teaching me how to have fun, before it was too late, and everything else. See you all on the dancefloor.

LAY OUT YOUR UNREST

www.ingramcontent.com/pod-product-compliance
Lightning Source LLC
Chambersburg PA
CBHW070050040426
42331CB00034B/2982